BREAKING FREE

Surviving a Narcissist Co-Parent

By Adell Harris

DEDICATION

To the brave mothers fighting silent battles—Loving someone who turns out to be a narcissist is painful. Sharing a child with one? That's a whole different battlefield.

This book is for every woman who's cried herself to sleep, questioning her worth, trying to co-parent with a man who manipulates, gaslights, and controls. For the mothers doing their best with what little support they've had. For the women who stayed longer than they wanted to—and still found the strength to leave.

I wrote this for you.

For the women who want to heal, reclaim their power, and create a peaceful future for themselves and their children.

And you are not powerless.

TABLE OF CONTENTS

INTRODUCTION

Leaving a narcissistic partner is one of the hardest decisions a mother can make. It means stepping into the unknown, away from a cycle of manipulation and emotional abuse, and toward a life of safety and sanity. If you've picked up this book, chances are you have already taken that brave step – or you are considering it. Breaking Free: Surviving a Narcissistic Co-Parent was born from my personal journey of finding the courage to walk away and learning to navigate life as a co-parent with someone who thrived on control.

In the beginning, I didn't know if I could do it. The fear of retaliation, the doubt planted by years of gaslighting, and the worry over how my child would fare weighed heavily on me. Narcissists have a way of making you feel powerless and dependent. My ex-partner's voice echoed in my head, telling me I'd fail on my own and that I was overreacting to his behavior. Perhaps you have heard similar words. Let me assure you: those words are lies designed to keep you under their thumb.

This book is not about legal strategies or clinical definitions alone – though we will discuss the practical aspects of dealing with custody and boundaries. It is also about healing, empowerment, and the emotional journey that comes with breaking free. Each chapter combines insights I learned through hard experience, advice from professionals that guided me, and the voices of fellow survivors who have walked this path. You'll find that you are far from alone; many women have faced a narcissistic co-parent and emerged stronger than ever.

As you read through these pages, remember that your story is your own. You may nod along with some parts and find others less applicable – and that's okay. Take what resonates with you. Use the journal prompts at the end of each chapter to reflect on your experiences and feelings. Speak the affirmations out loud or write them down; they are there to remind you of your strength and worth when times get tough.

Above all, Breaking Free: Surviving a Narcissistic Co-Parent is a companion for your journey. Think of it as a friend who has been through it and is here to offer understanding and practical tools. Whether you are
freshly separated or years into co-parenting, my hope is that this book will provide you with guidance, comfort, and the reaffirmation that you are indeed capable of raising your children in an environment of love and stability.

You've already shown tremendous courage by choosing a healthier path. Now, let's walk that path together.

CHAPTER 1

The Charm Before the Storm

"He didn't fall in love with you. He fell in love with your light—
and then tried to put it out."

The Charm Before the Storm

He was everything you thought you wanted.

Attentive. Charismatic. Charming. The kind of man who made you feel like the most important woman in the world. He came in strong—texting you every morning, calling every night, reminding you how special you were, how different you were from anyone else he had ever met. He studied you, mirrored your values, your faith, your language, your dreams. You didn't feel suspicious—you felt seen.

It didn't feel like a red flag. It felt like a fairytale.

You were a woman ready for love. Maybe you were tired of surface-level connections. Maybe you were healing from something else. Maybe you thought, *Finally, someone who understands me. Someone who really wants me.*

But here's the hard truth many of us never say out loud:
Narcissists don't choose weak women. They choose strong women—then work to dismantle them.

Recognizing the Love Bombing Phase

The love bombing was intense. Overwhelming, even. He moved fast—talking about forever, making promises, maybe even introducing you to his family early or mentioning kids before you really knew each other.

He may have said:
- *"I've never felt this way before."*
- *"I just know you're my person."*
- *"I would never hurt you."*

And he didn't just say it. He showed it. Flowers, surprise gifts, weekend getaways, spiritual conversations, maybe even talking about marriage within months or weeks. You were swept into a romance that made everything else fade.

That's the thing about love bombing—it's not love. Its control disguised as affection. It's a trap dressed up as destiny.

And it works because you're human. Because your heart is open. Because you're someone who believes in the good in people—and narcissists count on that.

When Things Started to Shift

At first, it was subtle.
Maybe it was the way he rolled his eyes when you shared something personal. Or how he suddenly got irritated when you didn't answer a call right away. Or how he became cold after a good day—leaving you confused, wondering what you did wrong.

You started noticing:
- He joked at your expense—but didn't like being teased himself.
- He gave you the silent treatment if you set a boundary.
- He said *"you're so sensitive"* whenever you spoke up.

Then came the hot-and-cold cycles. He'd pull away, then come back with a grand gesture. He created emotional whiplash—and you started working harder just to get back to the "good version" of him. The one you missed. The one who disappeared just as quickly as he arrived.

And when you confronted him? He flipped it. Now you were the problem.
"You're crazy."
"You're imagining things."

"You're trying to sabotage us."
You started walking on eggshells. And slowly, your confidence started to crack.

The Confusion Cycle

One of the hardest parts of this stage is the **cognitive dissonance**—holding two conflicting beliefs in your mind at once:
- *"He loves me. He's just stressed right now."*
- *"That didn't feel right, but maybe I'm overthinking."*

It's the internal tug-of-war between who you *thought* he was and how he's starting to make you feel.

You might've said things like:
- *"Every couple has problems."*
- *"He's been through a lot, I need to be patient."*
- *"Maybe I'm just not used to being loved."*

But here's the truth: **love doesn't feel like confusion. Love doesn't hurt you on purpose and call it passion.**

Red Flags You Missed (And Why It's Not Your Fault)

You may look back now and ask, *how didn't I see it?*

But real talk? You probably *did* feel it.

You felt it in your gut. In your nervous system. In the way your body started to tense before his name popped up on your phone. In the way your joy dimmed just a little more each time he "joked" about you, ignored your needs, or flipped the script after doing something wrong.

You didn't miss the red flags—you *overrode them*, because you were taught that love meant sacrifice. That love was hard work. That it was your job to hold the relationship together

But here's what those early red flags might've looked like:

- He blamed all his exes and had no accountability.
- He moved fast and pressured intimacy.
- He was charming in public, but moody and controlling in private.
- He love-bombed you, then withdrew affection to keep you guessing.
- He always had an excuse for disrespecting your time, your feelings, or your boundaries.

You ignored them because you wanted to believe the best.
That's not weakness. That's love. And you are not wrong for loving.
You were manipulated. And that's on *him*—not you.

How They Target Women Like You

Let's be very clear: this man didn't love you for your heart. He wanted your *light*—and when he saw he couldn't own it, he tried to dim it. Narcissists seek out:

- Strong, compassionate women with empathy
- Women who've overcome trauma but are still healing
- Women with something to lose—children, careers, community

Why? Because your strength makes him feel powerful when he conquers it.

He didn't fall for your flaws. He fell for your softness, your resilience, your ability to forgive. And then he used those qualities against you.

You didn't "fall for a narcissist."
You were *targeted* by one.

Journal Prompts

1. What were three early behaviors that made you uncomfortable, but you dismissed or excused?
2. In what ways did you abandon your own needs or intuition to "keep the peace"?
3. How would you comfort a friend who went through what you did?

Affirmations

- I forgive myself for the ways I silenced my own voice. I am listening to her now.
- I was not fooled. I was loving—and love should never be punished.
- The person who manipulated me does not define my worth. I reclaim my voice and my power.

NOTES

NOTES

CHAPTER 2

Understanding Narcissism

"You're not crazy. You're being conditioned to question your own reality."

Understanding Narcissism

Before you can survive a narcissist, you have to understand how they operate. Otherwise, you'll keep applying normal logic to someone who

doesn't live by normal rules—and every time, you'll walk away feeling confused, exhausted, and defeated.

Let's be clear: narcissists aren't just arrogant or self-absorbed. This goes deeper. This is about power, control, and manipulation disguised as love. And when you share a child with someone like this, the stakes—and the scars—are higher.

Traits of a Narcissist

Most narcissists won't walk into your life announcing who they are. They don't look like monsters. In fact, they often appear successful, generous, confident, and magnetic. They know how to "perform" in public. But behind closed doors, they reveal their true nature.

Some of the most common narcissistic traits include:
- A grandiose sense of self-importance ("I'm better than everyone else.")
- A constant need for admiration and validation
- A lack of empathy for how others feel
- A tendency to manipulate, guilt, or intimidate to get their way
- Extreme sensitivity to criticism—real or imagined
- Shifting blame when held accountable
- Seeing others (including children) as tools or extensions of themselves

They thrive on chaos and control. The more confused and unstable you are, the more power they feel.
But the most confusing part?

Sometimes, they can be really good at pretending to care.

One day they're gaslighting you, the next they're love bombing you again—apologizing, saying they miss you, buying your child a gift. It's a mind game. A cycle of emotional highs and lows meant to keep you hooked.

Narcissism vs. Narcissistic Personality Disorder (NPD)

It's important to understand the difference between someone who acts narcissistically and someone with **Narcissistic Personality Disorder (NPD)**.

Narcissistic traits can show up in anyone at times—especially under stress or in relationships. But NPD is a diagnosed mental health disorder marked by a long-term pattern of dysfunctional thinking, behavior, and emotional regulation.

According to the DSM-5, a person with NPD will exhibit at least five of the following:
- Fantasies of unlimited success, power, brilliance, or beauty
- Belief that they are special and can only be understood by other "high-status" people
- A constant need for admiration
- A sense of entitlement
- Exploitation of others for personal gain
- Lack of empathy
- Envy of others or belief that others are envious of them
- Arrogant, haughty behavior

But here's the kicker: **most narcissists will never get diagnosed**—because they rarely believe they have a problem. And even if they do see a therapist, they often manipulate the session to gain sympathy or play the victim.

Real-Life Example: "He Made Me the Villain"
One mother I spoke with shared this:

"We went to couples counseling after he cheated, and he told the therapist that I was cold and emotionally unavailable. That I had control issues. I was sitting there stunned, like—what?! I'd been walking on eggshells for years. He turned everything upside down, and the therapist, not knowing the full picture, started focusing on *my* communication issues. I left that session feeling ashamed—and more confused than ever."

That's how narcissists work. They flip the script, and if you don't understand how they operate, you will start to believe it's your fault.

How Narcissists Use Children as Pawns

This part hurts the most.

When you share a child with a narcissist, parenting becomes a battlefield. It's not about love—it's about control. And your child? They become the chess piece he uses to keep access to you.

Ways narcissistic co-parents use children to manipulate:
- **Weaponizing visitation** – canceling last-minute or showing up unexpectedly to assert dominance.
- **Using your child as a messenger** – *"Tell your mom I said…"*
- **Interrogating the child after visits** – trying to find out about your personal life.
- **Love bombing the child** – gifts, attention, over-the-top displays to seem like the "fun parent" while you do the real work.
- **Withholding support** – financially, emotionally, logistically— to cause stress.

They don't do this because they love the child. They do it to punish you. To pull you back into communication. To reassert control over the one area of your life they still feel entitled to: **your motherhood.**

Why You Stayed So Long

Let's take a deep breath here.

This chapter is heavy. And maybe as you're reading it, your heart hurts. Because it's bringing up memories you buried. Or making sense of things you've blamed yourself for.

You stayed because you *hoped*.

You stayed because he wasn't all bad—at least not at first. You stayed because he made you feel like he *needed* you. Because you didn't want your child to grow up without a father. Because you believed in the version of him that existed *before* the mask slipped.

You stayed because you wanted to fix it. Make it work. Love him into healing.

That doesn't make you foolish. That makes you human. That makes you kind. That makes you someone who saw potential and wanted a family.

But here's what no one tells you: **you can't out-love someone's disorder.**

You can't heal someone who doesn't think they're broken.

Stop Looking for Closure. Start Looking for Truth.

One of the most dangerous myths we're fed is that closure comes from the person who hurt us.

But narcissists don't give closure. They give confusion.

They want you to stay stuck. Stay questioning. Stay trying to get answers.

Because while you're doing that, you're still emotionally tethered to them.

Let go of the fantasy that he'll ever say:
- *"I'm sorry."*
- *"It was my fault."*
- *"You didn't deserve that."*

Your healing cannot wait on his accountability.

Closure comes from clarity.

Clarity that he was never going to be the man you needed him to be.

Clarity that you are not broken—you were abused.

Clarity that you have the power now. Not him.

Journal Prompts

1. In what ways did the narcissist in your life use charm, confusion, or guilt to keep you attached?
2. What have you learned about narcissistic behavior that has helped you begin to release blame?
3. What does closure look like for *you*—without expecting anything from him?

Affirmations

- I no longer confuse control with care. I know the difference between attention and love.
- I will not chase closure from someone who broke me. My healing starts with truth.
- I am no longer a pawn in his game. I reclaim my voice, my
- worth, and my future.

NOTES

NOTES

CHAPTER 3

The Emotional Rollercoaster

"Some days you're numb. Other days, you're drowning in emotions you can't even name."

The Emotional Rollercoaster

Being emotionally tied to a narcissist—especially when you share a child—feels like you're on a ride you didn't agree to board. You hold on tightly, hoping for stillness, but all you get are highs that never last and lows that pull you under.

One day he's telling you he "misses his family." The next, he's accusing you of alienating the child. One moment he's charming in front of others. The next, he's attacking you with a barrage of texts or cold silence that cuts deeper than words.

It's not love. It's manipulation. And it leaves you questioning everything—especially yourself.

Gaslighting, Guilt-Tripping, and Emotional Abuse

Narcissistic abuse isn't always loud. It's often quiet. Subtle. So subtle that it slips past your defenses. It starts with little digs. A look that says you're stupid.
A joke that cuts a little too deep. A denial of something you clearly remember happening.

It's not always what they say—it's how they **deny your reality**.

You hear things like:
- *"That never happened."*
- *"You're too sensitive."*
- *"You always make things bigger than they are."*
- *"You're imagining things again."*

At first, you argue. You defend yourself. You try to prove your truth. But over time, something dangerous starts to happen:

You begin to doubt your own mind.

You re-read texts to check if you overreacted. You ask friends if your feelings are valid. You question your instincts, your memory, your sanity.

And then comes the guilt-tripping.

He tells you:
- *"You're making me out to be a bad father."*
- *"I'm trying, but you're impossible."*
- *"If you weren't so bitter, we could co-parent better."*

He uses your compassion against you.
He takes your tenderness and turns it into a weapon.
He convinces you that the problems are your fault—and that he's the one suffering.

This is how emotional abuse works.
It doesn't show up with bruises. It shows up in **self-doubt**, **isolation**, and **anxiety** that you can't explain.

The Emotional Impact on You

When you live in this emotional chaos long enough, you begin to change. Not because you're weak—but because you're trying to survive.

You might feel:
- Like you're "too much" for having normal emotions
- Numb, flat, or emotionally detached—even from people who love you
- Overwhelmed by small tasks that once felt easy
- Physically sick from the stress (headaches, stomach issues, insomnia)
- Trapped between rage and guilt—never knowing which version of you will show up today

And the worst part? Everyone else might think you're fine.
You're still functioning. You're still parenting. You still smile in public.
But inside, you feel like you're unraveling.

That's the cost of emotional abuse. It lives in your nervous system.
You flinch at certain tones of voice.
You brace for attacks when your phone dings.
You stop trusting yourself—even though you were right all along.

How It Affects Your Child

You may think you're hiding it well. That you're shielding your child from the chaos. But children are **deeply intuitive**. They pick up on energy, tone, silence, fear.

Even if they don't understand the full dynamic, they *feel* it.

You may notice:
- Your child becomes quiet or withdrawn after visits
- They say things that sound like your ex's voice—not theirs ("Mommy's always angry")
- They start caretaking you emotionally—checking to see if you're okay
- They exhibit anxiety, aggression, regression, or sleep issues

Narcissistic co-parents often triangulate children to create loyalty conflicts. They subtly suggest that *you* are the difficult one. They play victim. They over-indulge your child with gifts or freedom to become the "fun parent."

But underneath it all, your child is confused.
They're being pulled between truth and manipulation.
And they're looking to **you** to understand what safety really feels like.

The Ping-Pong of Emotion

You may go back and forth emotionally in ways that feel disorienting:
- **Anger** at how he treated you.
- **Guilt** for exposing your child to the relationship.
- **Hope** that he might change.
- **Fear** that he'll use the child to punish you.
- **Grief** for the family you thought you were building.
- **Shame** for staying too long.
- **Resentment** for how much energy he still takes from you.

This emotional rollercoaster is real. It's not a weakness.
It's a natural result of being entangled with someone who emotionally abused you while pretending to love you.

Why You're Not "Over It" Yet

You may hear well-meaning people say:
- "Just move on."
- "Don't let him get to you."
- "You're free now—why are you still upset?"

But healing from narcissistic abuse is not like healing from a regular breakup.
It's not just about letting go of someone.
It's about **rebuilding the parts of you that were slowly dismantled**.

And if you still share a child with this person, you don't get to walk away clean.
You're still tethered—through messages, drop-offs, scheduling, court.
It's not that you're stuck in the past.
It's that the past still echoes into your present.

This is why your healing must be intentional.
Because no one else knows how deep this wound goes.

Real-Life Reminder: You're Not Alone

Let me tell you something personal:
I used to think I was going crazy.

I'd reread our messages at 2 a.m., trying to understand how we got here. I'd cry in the car after dropping my child off, feeling like a failure. I'd tell myself it was my fault—maybe I was the problem. Maybe I was too emotional. Too dramatic. Too unforgiving.

But I wasn't crazy.
I was being gaslit.
I was emotionally exhausted.
I was a mother doing her best in an impossible situation. And so are you.

Journal Prompts

1. What emotions feel hardest to express when dealing with your narcissistic co-parent?
2. What triggers you emotionally—and what boundaries can help protect your peace?
3. In what ways are you showing up for your child *even while hurting*?

Affirmations

- My emotions are valid. I don't need to shrink them to make others comfortable.
- I am not crazy—I am healing from prolonged emotional abuse.
- I release guilt and claim peace. I deserve to feel safe, loved, and whole again.

NOTES

NOTES

CHAPTER 4

Boundaries Save Lives

"He will cross every line you don't clearly draw—and fiercely protect."

Boundaries Save Lives

When you share a child with a narcissist, boundaries become more than just a tool—they become a lifeline. They're not for punishment. They're not for revenge. They're for **protection**—yours and your child's.

Because here's the truth:
A narcissist doesn't want co-parenting. He wants control.
And the only way to stop him from running over your peace is to draw a line in the sand—and never budge.

Why Boundaries Feel So Hard

Let's acknowledge something first:
Setting boundaries when you've been emotionally abused can feel terrifying.
You've been conditioned to walk on eggshells. To keep the peace. To avoid "starting something."

You may fear:
- He'll lash out if you say no.
- He'll make your child suffer for your decision.
- He'll take you back to court out of spite.
- He'll paint you as uncooperative or bitter.

Those fears are real. Narcissists often do retaliate when they feel they're losing control. But what's even more dangerous than setting a boundary—is not having one at all.

No boundary = no protection.
No boundary = constant chaos.
No boundary = emotional and spiritual erosion.

You are not responsible for how he reacts.

You are only responsible for protecting your peace.

Setting Boundaries with a Narcissist

Here's the thing: healthy people might not *like* your boundary—but they'll respect it. A narcissist? He'll test it. He'll mock it. He'll accuse you of being difficult, dramatic, controlling.

Which is exactly why your boundaries need to be:
- **Clear**
- **Firm**
- **Non-negotiable**

Examples of essential boundaries:
- *"I will only communicate through a court-approved parenting app."*
- *"I will not engage in emotional conversations. All messages must stay child-focused."*
- *"Pickups and drop-offs will only happen at the designated neutral location."*
- *"If you are more than 15 minutes late, I will leave and document it."*

You don't need to justify your boundary.
You don't need his approval.
You're not asking—you're informing.

Enforcing Consequences (Without Drama)
This part is where many mothers struggle. Not because they're weak—but because they're exhausted.

You set a boundary…
He crosses it.
You don't want to deal with another fight.
So you let it slide.

But every time you don't enforce the consequence, the narcissist learns that your boundary is flexible. And he will keep pushing.

To enforce a boundary:
- **Stay neutral** – Don't argue or explain. Stick to the facts.
- **Document everything** – Keep a log of violations.
- **Follow through** – If you say you'll leave after 15 minutes, leave.
- **Don't emotionally react** – That's what he wants. He feeds on your distress.

Boundaries are not about *controlling* him. They're about **not letting him control you**.

Real Example: The Pickup Power Struggle

One mom shared this:

"My ex would constantly show up 30 minutes late to drop-offs, then act like *I* was the unreasonable one when I said something. I used to wait. I used to argue. I used to text him a dozen times asking where he was. Now? I wait 15 minutes, document it, and leave. No response. No argument. Just a record for the court."

That's what boundaries look like: calm, consistent, empowered action.

Protecting Your Peace Without Starting War
You might feel like setting boundaries means creating conflict—but the opposite is true. Boundaries create clarity. Conflict comes from constantly being pushed and pulled.

You don't have to:
- Defend yourself every time he accuses you of something false
- Answer every message or phone call
- Engage with every provocation
- Explain your choices beyond what's legally required

Peace is not passive. Peace is a decision.
And sometimes, peace looks like silence. Distance. Detachment.

You're not being cold.
You're being careful.
Because you've learned the hard way that not everyone deserves access to your energy.

If You're Worried He'll Use Boundaries Against You…

He might.

Narcissists love to say:
- *"She's keeping my child from me."*
- *"She refuses to communicate."*
- *"She's high-conflict."*

That's why documentation is key. Use tools like:
- **TalkingParents**
- **OurFamilyWizard**
- **Email with time-stamps**
- **Text screen captures saved to a secure drive**

Keep your communication brief, factual, and about the child only. Do not vent. Do not defend. Do not explain beyond what's required.

In court, **your consistency will speak louder than his chaos.**

Journal Prompts

1. What boundary have you been afraid to set with your co-parent—and what would it feel like to finally enforce it?
2. What lie did the narcissist make you believe about having needs or standards?
3. How does your body feel when your boundaries are respected versus violated?

Affirmations

- I do not owe anyone access to my peace. My boundaries are sacred.
- I can be firm without being cruel. I protect my energy without apology.
- His reactions are not my responsibility. My job is to stay rooted in truth and calm.

NOTES

NOTES

CHAPTER 5

The Legal and Custody Battle

"When you go to war with a narcissist in court, you learn fast: the truth doesn't always win—but preparation does."

The Legal and Custody Battle

Court is not a place most mothers want to be. But when you're co-parenting with a narcissist, it often becomes necessary. You're not just fighting for custody. You're fighting for your child's safety, your own peace, and your right to be believed in a system that often favors appearances over reality.

And nobody wears a mask better than a narcissist.

The Courtroom: A Narcissist's Stage

The courtroom is where your ex sees an opportunity—not for resolution, but for performance. He'll walk in dressed sharply, smiling confidently, maybe even with a new partner at his side. He'll speak in calm, calculated tones, playing the victim or the hero depending on what will win him favor. The judge sees a concerned father. You see the same manipulator who's been tormenting you behind closed doors.

That duality is devastating.

He'll accuse you of alienation. He'll lie with ease. He'll frame your boundaries as bitterness. And the worst part? The system often gives him the benefit of the doubt.

If you walk in unprepared, he will exploit every weakness. But if you walk in informed, calm, and backed by documentation, you shift the power.

This chapter is your legal survival guide—not just for the courtroom, but for the emotional battlefield that comes with it.

Documenting is Your Armor

You can't out-talk a narcissist. You can't out-charm him. But you *can* out-document him.

Start now. Even if you haven't filed yet. Even if you think you won't need it. Create a system that tracks every interaction. Include:
- Missed visits or late pickups
- Inappropriate or harassing messages
- Manipulative behaviors witnessed by others
- Your child's emotional reactions before and after visits
- Any medical, educational, or behavioral concerns you've had to handle alone

Apps like **OurFamilyWizard**, **TalkingParents**, or **CustodyXChange** allows you to store communication, log events, and export time-stamped reports admissible in court.

It's not about being vindictive—it's about protecting your child with facts. Narcissists lie. Records don't.

Choosing the Right Legal Representation

All lawyers are not created equal. You need one who understands the nuances of high-conflict custody—not just one who can draft papers.

Your lawyer should:
- Be unbothered by charm tactics and gaslighting
- Know how to identify patterns of emotional abuse
- Be willing to go to trial if necessary
- Help you create a detailed, enforceable parenting plan

Before hiring them, ask:
- Have you handled custody cases involving narcissistic behavior?
- How do you handle clients being falsely accused?
- Can you help me establish communication boundaries in court orders?

This is not just a custody issue. It's a psychological chess match. You need a lawyer who sees the whole board.

Strategies for Family Court

Family court is not fair. It's designed for compromise, not conflict. That's why dealing with a narcissist can feel like playing by rules that don't exist.

Here's what helps:
- **Stay emotionless:** Narcissists bait you to react so they can call you "unstable." Stay grounded and neutral.
- **Stick to facts:** Use "I" statements. Be brief, clear, and specific. "On March 15, he missed pickup by two hours," not "He's always late."
- **Have a support person:** Bring a calm friend or advocate to court. Someone who can ground you and remind you of your truth.
- **Expect lies:** He may lie under oath. Expect it. Don't spiral. You're not there to fight fiction—you're there to present facts.

Remember: Family court is a marathon, not a sprint. Don't let one hearing shake your resolve.

Creating a Bulletproof Parenting Plan

A vague parenting plan is a narcissist's playground. The more specific your court orders, the less room there is for manipulation.

Include:
- Exact exchange times and locations
- Communication rules (via app only, no phone calls)
- Boundaries around third-party involvement (who can pick up, supervise, etc.)
- Detailed holiday/vacation schedules
- Clauses for makeup time or consequences for missed visits

Push for **parallel parenting** language if co-parenting proves toxic. This allows minimal communication and limits joint decision-making.

The Emotional Toll of Legal Warfare

You may walk out of court feeling defeated, even when you win. Why? Because fighting for your child against someone who should love them too is traumatic.

You feel exposed. Invalidated. Sometimes blamed.

But you're not crazy for needing legal protection. You're not dramatic for wanting peace. And you're not wrong for saying, "Enough."

You are doing what mothers have done since the beginning of time— fighting for your child's safety. Only now, you're doing it in a system that doesn't always understand emotional abuse.Stand firm in your truth. Even if the system is slow to catch up, your child will grow up knowing who protected them.

Journal Prompts

1. What emotions does the thought of going to court bring up for you—and where do those feelings come from?
2. How can documenting your ex's behavior become a form of empowerment instead of fear?
3. If you could speak in court with full confidence and power, what is the one truth you'd want the judge to understand about your situation?

Affirmations

- I will not let his lies define my truth. I speak with clarity, and I am rooted in evidence.
- I am not afraid of the system. I am prepared, protected, and powerful.
- Even if the judge doesn't see it today—my child will know I fought for their peace.

NOTES

NOTES

CHAPTER 6

Coping, Healing, and Growing

"You didn't just survive him. Now it's time to come home to yourself."

Coping, Healing, and Growing

You've fought so many battles—some in courtrooms, some behind closed doors, and many in your own mind. You've carried the weight of a broken relationship, a child's needs, and your own pain. And now, you're standing in the space between survival and healing.

This space can be quiet—but it's not empty. It's sacred. It's where the real work begins.

After leaving a narcissist, your world doesn't magically go back to normal. You're not just recovering from a breakup. You're untangling yourself from a person who deliberately tried to erase you.

So if you're still struggling—still crying, still anxious, still unsure of who you are—that's not failure. That's the beginning of your healing.

The Grief You Didn't Expect

Grief after narcissistic abuse is complicated. You're not just grieving the person—you're grieving the *hope* you had for who they could have been. You're grieving the family you wanted, the future you imagined, and the love you believed in.

And on top of that, you may still have to see him, talk to him, or send your child off to him.

It's like healing from a wound that keeps getting reopened.

Let yourself grieve:
• Grieve the woman you were before him.
• Grieve the way you silenced your voice to keep the peace.
• Grieve the time you can't get back.
But also, honor the fact that you're still standing. That's not just survival. That's strength.

Therapy, Journaling, and Support Systems

You don't have to be strong alone. In fact, healing accelerates when you let others witness your truth.

- **Therapy**: Find a trauma-informed therapist who understands narcissistic abuse. It's not just talk therapy—it's rewiring your nervous system to stop expecting danger.
- **Journaling**: Your journal doesn't judge. Write your rage. Your sadness. Your confusion. Your joy. It's a safe place where you don't need to filter or explain.
- **Support groups**: Whether online or in person, connect with other women who've lived it. You'll find strength in knowing you're not the only one.

The world may not always believe emotional abuse. But other survivors will. And they will remind you: your story matters.

Rebuilding Your Self-Esteem

Narcissists are experts at eroding your confidence. Every insult. Every silent treatment. Every moment they made you question your worth—it leaves a scar.

But self-worth can be rebuilt.

Start small:
- Speak kindly to yourself, especially on the hard days.
- Celebrate the tiny wins: a boundary kept, a night of rest, a moment of peace.
- Look in the mirror and find one thing to admire—even if it's just your eyes, your laugh, your resilience.
- Stop apologizing for things that require no apology: your boundaries, your no, your silence.

You don't need to return to the woman you were before him. That version of you didn't know what she knows now.

You are becoming someone wiser, stronger, and more rooted in self-love than ever before.

Healing While Mothering

This is one of the hardest parts—healing while still showing up for your child. There's no pause button. You're comforting them through nightmares while quietly having your own. You're helping with homework while carrying the weight of your trauma.

You may feel like you're faking it. You're not.

Every time you choose peace over chaos, calm over conflict, or rest over revenge—you're modeling healing.

Let your child see your humanity. Say:
- "Mommy's feeling sad today, but I'm okay."
- "Sometimes big feelings are hard, but I'm learning how to handle them."
- "You can talk to me about anything, just like I'm learning to talk about my feelings too."

You're not just raising them—you're reparenting yourself. And every gentle choice is a step toward breaking the cycle.

Redefining Who You Are

You are not what he called you. You are not your trauma. You are not just "a single mom." You are a woman who made a brave, life-altering decision to walk away from abuse.

Now, you get to decide who you are:
- Are you creative? Start painting again.
- Are you nurturing? Plant something.
- Are you funny? Dance, joke, watch comedies.
- Are you passionate? Reconnect with your purpose.

Healing is not about erasing what happened. It's about rediscovering the parts of you that were buried under his control—and bringing them back to life.

Journal Prompts

1. What part of yourself do you miss most—and what would it look like to nurture that part again, even in a small way?
2. How has being a mother while healing changed your definition of strength?
3. What is one limiting belief you adopted during the relationship—and what is the truth you're ready to replace it with?

Affirmations

- I am not behind—I am right on time in my healing.
- Even on my hardest days, I am showing up with courage, love, and intention.
- I am not just surviving. I am returning to myself—one choice, one breath, one day at a time.

NOTES

CHAPTER 7

Co-Parenting vs. Parallel Parenting

"You cannot co-parent with someone who is still trying to control or destroy you. That's not co-parenting—it's surviving."

Co-Parenting vs. Parallel Parenting

There's a fantasy we're all sold: two mature adults, putting aside their issues, working together for the well-being of the child. That's co-parenting. And for some people, it works beautifully.

But if your child's other parent is a narcissist, that fantasy becomes a nightmare.

Because to co-parent, there must be mutual respect, shared goals, and emotional maturity.

A narcissist brings none of that.

Instead, he brings chaos—undermining, manipulation, pettiness, and control masked as concern.

So, let's name the truth: **co-parenting with a narcissist is not only unrealistic, it's dangerous to your peace**. That's where **parallel parenting** comes in—not as a last resort, but as a radical act of self-preservation.

Why Co-Parenting Doesn't Work With a Narcissist

You may have tried. Maybe you believed that, for the child's sake, you could find some common ground. Maybe you agreed to flexible arrangements, shared decisions, or frequent check-ins.

But here's what often happens:
- He uses communication as a tool to harass, guilt-trip, or provoke you.
- He contradicts your parenting in front of the child to confuse and control.
- He violates agreements casually and expects you to "be the bigger person."
- He turns every negotiation into a power struggle.

It's not parenting—it's psychological warfare.

And every time you try to cooperate, he weaponizes it.

The moment you stop dancing to that rhythm, he accuses you of being "difficult," "uncooperative," or "vindictive."

It's exhausting. And worse—it's unhealthy for your child to witness a parenting dynamic full of tension, conflict, and fear.

What is Parallel Parenting?

Parallel parenting is not giving up—it's letting go of the fantasy and embracing what's real. It's a structured, low-contact approach that allows both parents to raise the child independently, without emotional entanglement or forced collaboration.

It's a method designed to **reduce conflict, protect your mental health**, and **shield your child from toxic tension**.

Here's what it looks like:
- **All communication is written**, usually through a court-monitored app like TalkingParents or OurFamilyWizard.
- **Drop-offs and pickups are structured**—often at neutral locations or through third parties.
- **There are no shared decisions** unless absolutely necessary. You parent on your time, and he parents on his.
- **You stick to court orders—no flexibility, no verbal agreements.**
- **You document everything.**

This isn't cold—it's clear.

This isn't punishing him—it's protecting you.

The Emotional Shift: From Pleasing to Protecting

Many mothers feel guilt when they step away from "co-parenting" and into parallel parenting. You may feel like you're being uncooperative. That you're somehow failing your child by not making it work.

But ask yourself: **How is it helping your child to witness you being disrespected and disregarded over and over again?**

Children are emotionally safer in two separate, peaceful households than one where control, fear, and conflict dominate every exchange.

Parallel parenting is a form of love. It says:
"I care too much about my child—and myself—to keep trying to cooperate with someone who refuses to be respectful."

Practical Tools for Parallel Parenting

Here are strategies to put parallel parenting into action:
- **Keep all communication factual, brief, and necessary.** No emotions. No explanations.
  Example: *"Per the agreement, pickup is at 3:00 p.m. at the community center."*
- **Do not respond to baiting.** If he sends a long, insulting message, respond only to what's necessary—or not at all.
- **Use shared calendars or apps** to avoid direct communication.
- **Establish boundaries around decision-making.**
  Example: *"During my time, I'll handle school-related issues. Please direct school concerns to me via email."*
- **Involve third parties** when necessary. This might include therapists, mediators, or court-appointed parenting coordinators.
- **Let go of the illusion of control.** You cannot change how he parents. You can only influence what happens in your home.

Focusing on What You Can Control

This is hard—but it's also freeing.

You cannot control:
- How he behaves
- What he says to others
- Whether he follows through

You *can* control:
- Your boundaries
- Your energy
- Your parenting choices
- Your response (or lack thereof)

And most importantly—you can control the **emotional climate in your home**. That's where your power lives.

Your Home is the Healing Ground

Your child doesn't need both parents to be emotionally healthy to thrive. **They need at least one parent who is stable, loving, and safe.**

That's you.

In your home, you get to model:
- Emotional intelligence
- Respectful communication
- Boundaries without cruelty
- Love without manipulation

You get to be the example. You get to break the cycle. You get to give your child what you didn't always have: **a safe space.**

Journal Prompts

1. What have you been trying to "make work" with your ex that you now realize is no longer healthy for you or your child?
2. What would your life look like if your peace was protected by structure instead of constant compromise?
3. How can you redefine success in parenting—based on your values, not his reactions?

Affirmations

- I no longer engage in power struggles. I protect my peace and my child's peace with strength and clarity.
- I am not obligated to create harmony with someone who brings chaos. Distance is not cruelty—it's wisdom.
- My child learns what love looks like by watching me honor myself.

NOTES

NOTES

CHAPTER 8

Protecting Your Child

"You can't control the narcissist—but you can raise a child who knows love, truth, and safety."

Protecting Your Child

If you've made it this far, it's because you are not just a survivor—you're a protector. A mother with fire in her soul and love in her bones. You're trying to do what feels impossible: shield your child from the emotional damage of someone they are biologically connected to.

You're watching your child smile as they go off to visit a parent you know is harmful. You're pretending everything is okay when your insides scream, *This isn't right*. And through it all, you're carrying the invisible burden of trying to protect someone from a storm you didn't create.

Let's start by saying this clearly: **you are doing more than most will ever understand.** And even when it doesn't feel like enough—you are making a difference.

The Truth About Narcissistic Parenting

A narcissist doesn't see their child as a separate, sacred human being. They see them as:
- A reflection of their ego
- A pawn in their power games
- A tool for revenge
- A symbol of control

This shows up in ways that are hard to prove—but devastating to witness:
- Overindulging the child to look like the "fun parent"
- Undermining your rules or badmouthing you behind your back
- Using the child as a messenger or spy
- Withholding affection to punish or manipulate
- Forcing the child to "choose sides" emotionally

Your child may come home confused, angry, or shut down—and you're left to pick up the pieces.

It's heartbreaking. But you are not powerless.

Emotional Armor: Teaching Your Child Emotional Intelligence

Your child may not have the words to describe what's happening— but they feel it. They notice the tension. The mixed messages. The emotional instability.

That's why emotional intelligence is one of your greatest tools.

Start small:
- Ask open-ended questions: "How did that make you feel?"
- Name emotions together: "It sounds like you're feeling frustrated. Is that right?"
- Validate their feelings, even if you don't agree: "It's okay to feel confused or mad."
- Offer safe language: "Sometimes grown-ups say or do things that don't feel good. That's not your fault."

When your child feels *seen* and *safe*, they learn to trust their instincts. They learn that love is not supposed to hurt. And most importantly— they learn that their voice matters.

What Not to Say: Staying Truthful Without Alienating
You don't have to sugarcoat. But you also don't need to speak badly about your child's other parent.

Find the middle ground. Be honest without projecting your hurt:
- Instead of "Your dad is a liar," say:
"Sometimes people say things that aren't true. If you ever feel unsure, we can talk about it."
- Instead of "He doesn't really love you," say:

"Real love means showing up with respect and kindness. You deserve that kind of love."

- Instead of "He's trying to turn you against me," say:
"I'll always love you no matter what anyone else says. You never have to choose between us."

Your child will grow up and put the pieces together on their own. Your job is to create a safe place where the truth can land gently—when they're ready to see it.

Building a Safe Emotional Environment at Home

Your home is more than four walls—it's a sanctuary. And while you can't control what happens in the other home, you *can* create:
- Predictable routines
- Emotional availability
- Gentle discipline rooted in respect
- Space to decompress after visits
- Open communication without fear of punishment

Your child may be exposed to emotional manipulation. But when they come back to *your* space, they need consistency, calm, and care.

And don't underestimate the power of play, laughter, and quiet moments. These are healing rituals too.

Signs Your Child May Be Struggling

Kids don't always say, "I'm being emotionally abused." But they will show you:
- Sudden mood swings or withdrawal
- Repeating phrases they clearly didn't come up with
- Defending the narcissistic parent aggressively
- Sleep issues, stomachaches, or anxiety
- Acting out or shutting down after visitation

If something feels *off*, trust your instincts. Journal the changes. Bring them to your therapist or attorney. Seek an evaluation if needed. The goal is not to label your child—but to support them early.

Advocating Without Guilt

You might worry that you're "making it worse" by pushing for court intervention, therapy, or evaluations.

But listen carefully, Mama: **protecting your child emotionally is not revenge—it's responsibility**.

If you see patterns of psychological harm, don't wait for a crisis. Be the voice they can't use yet. Document everything. Request a **Guardian ad Litem**, a **custody evaluator**, or **court-ordered therapy** if necessary.

You don't need to wait until your child is broken to fight for their well-being.

You're Not Just Raising a Child—You're Breaking a Cycle

Every time you model calm in the face of chaos…
Every time you listen without judgment…
Every time you validate your child's feelings when the other parent dismisses them…
You are changing the narrative.

You are teaching your child:
- •How to name what's not okay
- How to choose peace over performance
- How to trust themselves, even when others try to distort the truth

That's the kind of parenting that heals generations.

Journal Prompts

1. What are three ways you can reinforce emotional safety for your child at home—even after visits with their other parent?
2. What do you wish someone had told you as a child when things felt confusing or unsafe? Can you offer that to your child now?
3. How have you already shown up as your child's protector, even when no one else saw it? What strength does that reveal in you?

Affirmations

- I am a safe place for my child. I protect, I nurture, and I lead with love and clarity.
- Even if I cannot control every environment, I can create one that heals.
- My child will grow up knowing what truth, safety, and love feel like—because of me.

NOTES

NOTES

CHAPTER 9

Life After the Narcissist

"You thought survival was the goal. But peace—that's the real reward."

Life After the Narcissist

There's something strange about freedom after abuse.

You think you'll feel relief. And maybe you do, at first. But soon, a different emotion creeps in—disorientation. You've spent so long bracing for the next emotional blow, navigating manipulation, watching your back, walking on eggshells.

And now… it's quiet.

At first, that silence feels unnatural. You may even feel guilty for the calm. That's trauma talking. That's your nervous system still living in survival mode.

But as the quiet settles, something beautiful starts to bloom: your spirit. Your identity. Your peace.

This chapter is about reclaiming joy after chaos. Not just surviving—but *thriving*.

The Emotional Hangover

Even after the narcissist is physically gone, their presence can linger.
- You may hear their voice in your head, second-guessing your decisions.
- You may flinch when your phone buzzes.
- You may feel unworthy of love or too "damaged" to start over.
- You may question whether your peace is even real.

That's all normal. It's part of the decompression process. You've been gaslit, criticized, and emotionally battered. You're not just learning how to live again—you're learning how to feel safe inside your own mind.

Take it slow. Your healing doesn't have to look like glowing overnight. It might look like:
- Taking a nap without guilt
- Laughing without worry
- Trusting your instincts again
- Saying "no" without explanation

Every moment of peace is a rebellion against the chaos you once accepted.

Dating Again (If and When You're Ready)

There's no pressure to date. Your value isn't determined by who wants you.
But if you choose to open your heart again—do it from a place of *wholeness*, not from a place of needing to be rescued.

Here's what to keep in mind:
- **Go slow.** You're not in a rush. Healthy love doesn't move at lightning speed.
- **Stay grounded in your intuition.** If something feels off, trust that.
- **Ask real questions.** Not just "Do I like them?" but "Do I feel safe with them?"
- **Notice how you feel around them.** Are you shrinking? Overexplaining? Walking on eggshells again?

You don't need to be perfect to be loved. But you do need to love yourself enough not to settle for crumbs just because it's not chaos.

And remember: the right person won't be intimidated by your boundaries—they'll respect them.

Thriving in Your Peace

Peace might feel foreign. You may mistake it for boredom at first. But peace is *not* the absence of excitement—it's the absence of fear.

Here's what thriving might look like:
- Waking up and feeling calm, instead of dreading the day
- Smiling because you want to—not because someone demands it
- Feeling safe to rest, eat, cry, and create
- Parenting with joy instead of fear
- Making choices that align with your values—not his control

You get to build a life that reflects *you* now. Not the woman you had to be to survive. But the woman you are becoming.

Being the Example Your Child Needs

Your healing is not just for you—it's for your child. They are watching you more than they are listening to you.

- When they see you: Speak with confidence
- Set boundaries and enforce them
- Cry and recover
- Apologize when you're wrong
- Celebrate your wins

They are learning that healing is possible. That strength is not perfection. That safety is a birthright—not something earned through pleasing others.

You are not just breaking a cycle. You are building a legacy.

The Beauty of Starting Over

There's grief in starting over. But there's also beauty.

You get to:
- Redefine motherhood on your terms
- Decorate your home with peace and freedom
- Laugh again—deep, from-the-gut laughter
- Eat what you like, watch what you want, wear what makes you feel beautiful
- Be fully, unapologetically you

You are not too late. You are not too broken. You are not too anything.

You are *ready*.

Journal Prompts

- What does peace feel like in your body, and how can you create more of it in your daily routine?
- If you could speak to the future version of yourself five years from now, what do you hope she's doing, feeling, and believing about herself?
- How do you define "thriving" now—and how is that different from when you were in survival mode?

Affirmations

- I am allowed to rest. I am allowed to laugh. I am allowed to build a life that reflects my freedom.
- I am not my past—I am the author of my future.
- Peace is not a luxury. It is my new foundation. And I rise from it, every day.

NOTES

CHAPTER 10
Letters to the Women
"If you're still in the storm, this chapter is for you."

Letters to the Women

You may be deep in it right now—feeling like no one sees you, like your voice is small, like every step forward is met with ten steps back.

Maybe you're still sharing a home. Maybe you've left, but his voice still lives in your head. Maybe you've won custody battles, but the war still rages inside your spirit. Maybe you haven't told anyone what's really happening because you don't even have the words yet.

This chapter is not about tools or strategies. This one is just for your heart.

To the Woman Who Hasn't Left Yet

You're not weak. You're not stupid. You're not failing your child.

You are calculating, planning, surviving. You are gathering strength while pretending everything's fine. You are keeping the peace in a war zone—and that takes courage most people will never understand.

If no one has told you lately:
- I believe you.
- You're not crazy.
- Love is not supposed to feel like fear.
- You are allowed to leave even if he doesn't hit you.
- You are still worthy, even if you've stayed longer than you wanted to.

When you are ready, you will leave. And when you do, we will be here—on the other side—waiting with arms open.

To the Woman Who Just Left

The hardest part isn't always walking out—it's staying gone.

You might be missing the highs. You might be questioning your own memory. You might feel like you can't breathe without him—even though he was the one choking your light.

You are not wrong for missing him. That's the trauma bond talking. That's your nervous system still untangling what love *should* feel like.

But hear me clearly:
Missing him doesn't mean you made a mistake.
Doubting yourself doesn't mean you should go back.
Feeling weak doesn't mean you aren't strong.

You are detoxing from manipulation. That's not weakness—it's healing.

Hold the line. Keep going. One hour at a time if you have to.

To the Mother Who's Still Fighting

Court cases. Mediation. Exchanges filled with tension. Passive-aggressive messages. Tears after pickup. Fear at every ding of your phone.

This is the battlefield no one prepares you for.

You are not dramatic. You are not overreacting. You are *at war with a man who wants to win—not co-parent*. And still—you show up. You comfort your child. You document. You breathe.

You are not just surviving him. You are protecting your child from the emotional storm he creates. And that, Mama, is holy work.

Stay grounded in your truth. Even when it feels like no one sees the whole picture—*you* know what's real.

To the Woman Who Feels Broken

There may be days when you don't recognize yourself.

You used to laugh more. Sleep better. Love deeper. Now you're tired, numb, guarded, afraid to trust—even your own instincts.

But you are not broken. You are becoming.

This pain is not the end of your story. It's the beginning of your return. Your voice is still inside you. Your joy is still reachable. Your spirit is still alive.

You don't have to rush to be "healed." Just keep showing up for yourself with tenderness and truth.

To the Woman Who's Ready to Rise

There will come a day—sooner than you think—when you'll wake up and realize you're not afraid anymore.

You won't jump at every sound. You won't overthink every message. You won't shrink to make others comfortable.

Instead, you'll look in the mirror and say: *"She's back."*

And your child will feel it too. They'll see your strength. They'll feel your peace. They'll learn, through you, that it's okay to leave what hurts—even if it's someone you once loved.

You are not just surviving this.
You are becoming the woman you were always meant to be.

And we are cheering for you—every step of the way.

Journal Prompts

1. What do you need to hear most right now—and how can you begin saying it to yourself?
2. Write a letter to the version of you who stayed. What compassion and understanding does she deserve?
3. If you believed—without a doubt—that peace and freedom were possible for you, what would you do next?

Affirmations

- I am not broken. I am healing. I am rising.
- Every day I choose truth over fear, I reclaim my life.
- I am becoming the woman I was always meant to be—and I am proud of her.

NOTES

ABOUT THE AUTHOR

Adell Harris is a writer, advocate, and survivor of narcissistic abuse who turned her personal healing journey into a mission to help other women find their voice. Through her powerful storytelling and practical tools, she empowers mothers to break the cycle of manipulation and reclaim their peace. Adell believes every woman has the right to raise her children in an environment free from emotional chaos.

www.ingramcontent.com/pod-product-compliance
Lightning Source LLC
Chambersburg PA
CBHW071539120626
46550CB00006B/2518